A MARK OF PERMANENCE

JUSTIN WATKINS

Up On Big Rock Poetry Series
SHIPWRECKT BOOKS PUBLISHING COMPANY
Minnesota

Cover chalkboard art by John Piacquadio
Cover & interior design by Shipwreckt Books

ISBN-13: 978-0-9990430-7-3
ISBN- ISBN-10: 0-9990430-7-2

A Mark of Permanence

Contents

Poems from Land and Water

He explains the importance of eating wild trout

You think me wildly coarse
That I embrace the muddy roots of earth
And lower my ear close to water
To encrimson my hands
And steal

How can one disfigure this living art you ask
And feast on the very canvas
How can one strike the pulsing gills
And push the dark knife into
The belly

The answer is known to some
These fish are not external to the world
They are an accumulation of rock and water
A path through periphyton and insect
To flesh

No heavy hand has made them more sacred
Than the flow that falls from stone
Indeed to bite the bones of this scaled vessel
Of the ancient water is the undying way
To bind oneself to it

Holy Water Road

We found a spined pig
High in a tree
A forager

Just off the two-track
Holy Water Road
Circa 1980

A wandering father
A son, quiet under
Hooded sweatshirt

The gray, orange of fall
And he asked me
Should I shoot it

That porcupine
Should I shoot it
Just there in the tree

And the decider
Slow to reply, then
Yeah, shoot it

Are you sure
Yeah, shoot it
From high in the tree

It fell loose and heavy
Obscure in leaf litter
And we walked on

Two feral dogs

Loped from the swamp
The sudden wild-eyed panting
Matted and fouled dark coats
Some ghoul's footmen

And we all perched above
In our time of smooth skin
Easy drinking easy movements
The unkillable youth

Now leaning over deck rails
Tracking the ragged beasts
Have you seen them before
Never he says

They trot loose patterns
Dark obscure ever-moving
And then shrieks from below
Shrieks rising and falling

In the burned-out yard
A dog mouthing a rabbit kit
One killing compression
Swallowing it whole

Stop them demand the women
As the demon dogs run circles
Tackling and crushing and swallowing
Stop them do something

And we understand the duty
But we just stare as a group
The whole nest now daylighted
Rabbits shrieking and dying

Jesus someone says
Do something is the chant
We stare: what can we do
What can one do about that

Snapping turtle

Dark heads of cloud
Gaseous gray forms
Heat lightning

The water a black glass plane
The great beast
Left to right in shallows

Studded shellback
Scaled and clawed feet
Webbed fans slowly reaching

I caught a big one like that
You say: back home on the river
Tailed'm and swung'm into the canoe

No real plan about what to do
I thought he'd be afraid of me
More flashes and deep thunder

I was wrong about that
You state flatly as the turtle rises
To the tension between water and air

Suspends in absolute stillness
And an audible exhalation
Some trading of breath with electric air
        An exhale or word unknown

Driftwood one-matcher

August
Sleeping on dredge islands
Hot sands
Nights alive with river fowl

Tall grass hummocks
Gray lumber and driftwood
A humble altar
Southeast into rising sun

The boy in the tent
He is my outbreathing
I guard the door
This and all days

Soon I will call his name
Bring him to the fire
To the first light
And the singing cranes

We found a cache of muskrat corpses

On the shoulder of the cliff
Twisted black desiccations
Strewn just over the guardrail

You wouldn’t believe how smooth
A rat fur can be
So smooth he said staring

The only thing that distinguished them
From reptile or bird
The bared orange teeth

As if lips peeled back
In recoil from the sun or piercing grass
A stilled grimace shaped in a drown trap

Corpses mingled with all brands of debris
Suppose they used a shovel from a truck bed
Pulled up and threw’m over he said

The carpenter

He has worked harder
And longer than most
His hands and visage
Are testament

His hearth and pantry
Are spartan humble
The windows quiet
Bedworks untouched

In a fireside bucket
Lumber remnants
All of them notepads
Dimensions counts angles
In thick carpenter pencil

Late nights of frosted pane
He leans low to stone
And feeds these tablatures
These gray inscriptions

Carefully one by one
Into fire: his life's work
Burning chapters of his world
To warm his silent house

Near Cherry Creek

Too many roosters is the issue
The problem we have to deal with
Hold this while I go grab ‘em

See how it’s dark there almost black
On the block and on the axe head
But boy is it bright on your hands

The running isn’t regular like they say
It’s floppy and circular, concentric
Like they’re tethered to a center pivot

Yeah wet feathers in warm water
Reduce to a fistful of quills and fibers
Easy to bury in a small hole

Other than that—grab those heads
I’ll take the meat to the workers
Blood’ll wash away on its own

Asking for permission to access private property

The well water is perfect
She kept coming back to that
The gray tatters of a dooryard
Her face slack with concession
Behind us horses picked up
And set down their hooves

And again: don't hurt my well
First visitors in how many years
And this is how I'm dressed
The oil stain on her farm coat
Had spread over her left breast
There covering her heart

Champing of the horses louder
This painful palpable tension
Wanting and not wanting us around
Became too much and she said
Okay just don't cut any fence
And it seemed an exhalation

Walking back to the car she stopped
By the blowing pole building doors
To justify her suspiciousness:
Bad things have happened around here
We turned to find her squinting in the sun
We don't socialize

The properties of water

On New Year's Day
Near the Laurentian Divide
We set a fire on a lake as truth
Things we can know for certain:
Wood heat ice flame steam water

And fish: which the youth address
Skewering light sucker minnows
Lowering them through ice
To list and fin and circle slowly
In cold silence

We are a semi-circle
Of drab matted clothing
Watching embers work downward
A dark wood matrix sinking
Pulling our minds toward

The properties of water
The Godhand that set them
Such that density increases
As it cools to four Celsius
And decreases thereon to ice

A hexagonal lattice saves the lakes
From freezing bottom up
And thus gives us time to stand
Together: dodging smoke and wind
Watching holes in ice

Two minnows die in the snow
Curling into aching C-shapes
Their red gills crystallize
And the boys holler at a flag
Come on little men says one

Hand over hand all feeling
A hookset and a tightness
A joining: flesh to flesh
Air and water through ice
The wolf of the water is laid low

We return to our altar
As the cold comes to the pike
Each head-to-tail writhing slower
Shorter, until its own water
Goes to ice

Walking at night on the river

The yellow dog trots in eagerness
In and out of our cone of sight
He has been known to kill rabbits
His old coat has been spattered with blood

The river is just visible in the closing dim
Its only sound is the fall at the abandoned mill
The path has been made a dark tunnel
Under an interlocked canopy of branches

The ground and leaves are wet
Footfalls are quiet and trees snuff words
This puts us on careful watch
Eyes always moving not trusting our ears

We meet a lone man heading north
Gray matted coat and head bowed
His face hidden and arms wrapped tight
He is obscured

After walking some distance we turn to look:
He has stopped at our point of meeting
Standing still head tilted
Watching us closely

Green sunfish

First day of middle school
Early morning rain
Gray windows
Soft drumming

And your lip trembling
At the tail of the dalmatian molly
Protruding from the mouth
Of the green sunfish

The predator:
No heart for an aquarium
Untamable just as we feared
And now lament

You are old enough
I sense you figuring
That you shouldn't cry
A boy at a threshold

I hold the fish gently
In spite of its sin
Your eyes down studying
Your fingers careful and forgiving

No we can't pull it out backward
Some tail spines come off in my hand
You see but look away
Staring into rain at the window

Dragging a deer through new snow

The wooded sideslope
A stark monochrome
Angular blacks
A mantle of white

The hunter between these
At careful progress
Downhill toward the ravine
Bare hands on antler

A pause for rest
His breath before him
And uphill the crimson trail made
The only curve and color

Story related over coffee

One gal did nothing but cut off their eyelids
754 heads per hour on a conveyor belt
She had a special knife for it

So that's a strong 1500 eyelids per hour
What in the hell for
Wouldn't 1500 eyelids equal about one ham

I don't recall how they used 'em
Think it was a sort of research or medical deal
Them bein' so thin and delicate

She had some nightmares I'd say
Seeing those faces all day I bet they just bled
Right through into night

Heads that were dead
But looked alive and awake eyes wide open
And she standing there holding the covers

At the Jeffers Petroglyphs Visitor Center

Outside in pink quartzite
Are hands of men
Not carved or painted
But pecked out
Marking the exit points
Of shamans who dove into rock
To trade tobacco for medicine

Inside, my son's hands
Wield a tomahawk
A globe of dark stone
Lashed to a handle
He struggles to manage it
His size and innocence
Refuse to support it

To the north is a fort
It was surrounded
Four hundred braves
Some held these tomahawks
Pumped them in defiance:
When men are hungry
They help themselves

And to the east is a town
It was besieged
Children were hidden
In corners of brick buildings
A ring of flaming ramparts

Set against those who would not
Eat their own dung

Never have I seen
Someone coming to kill me
No war party has crested
My rolling hill
Raising a terrible cry
Bearing down
In a roar of beating hooves

Nor have I leveled a gun
At another man
To proclaim that his home
Is now my home
But those things happened here
The feet and the hands
Are in the rock

They walked and touched
The prairie grass
Holding heavy tomahawks
Like this one
Which my son now replaces
As we move through double doors
Into the sunlight

Snowbank lake

The walk behind the shed is good
Game trails in balsam thickets
Only minor blowdown

There's an old Forest Service latrine
In the alder swamp
Stood it upright so you can see it

Found a survey monument
Probably quarter section marker
By a fire ring alongshore just east

Walked a long way real slow
Pausing to stoop low and watch
Looked good: balsam thickets and alders

We haven't seen a grouse in years she says
Used to be we'd hear 'em from the yard
Most days drumming on logs

We study the curling sauna smoke
The cold heavy lake water
Birch leaves gathering yellow around us

I eject brass-capped red shells into grass
We could hear 'em from the yard she says
Beating their wings in an old rhythm

Fence repair

Take the rotten boards down
Put 'em in the truck
Use these new ones to replace 'em

He set his hand on the roughcut lumber
Making for wood on wood
For his fingers were the knotted fir

Use the tape measure
Cut with the handsaw
There's no real trick to it

The boy hesitated
Searching for some further guidance
Perhaps a written word

But the man reassured him:
These are boards son
Real things in the world

The saw cuts across the grain
And the nails part the grain to hold tight
We make fences so horses don't run off

At this the boy nodded
Started for the cab
Found the steering wheel at eye level

The man stopped when the engine fired
His jeans stacked up at his boot tops
He waved once and walked off through the pasture

Beulah Township

The griffon he says
She picked up a scent
That shamblin old porky
Come on now let's go look

Walk around that birch
I say: look up and to the left
He disappears and then a shot
We all hear it breaking limbs

Falling
And then a pitchfork
A ferric tool of tines
I can't figure what God wanted

He says: with the porcupine
What good is it
They chew on trees is about all
And I've put some thought on it

The boy heaves it up into the dumpster
To keep it from the dogs
The fork still intact pinning it
Wheezing wheezing but no face

No eyes to meet
Only thick white quills arrayed
No face: just wheezing
And laborious turning of the head

Under the tines
Take that thing down
And now look away boys
He hefts a 4x4 timber

I've put some thought on it
And we have no rebuttal
The mound of quills now quiet
The men and boys receding into the pines

Whiskey at noon hour in camp

Alder birch spruce pine granite
The substance of the place
Was their review:
These words all spoken well

After time some laid down on caribou moss
Others watched the bay
The lone canoe at distance
Moving slowly on bright water

The hidden flat

Paleozoic Seas have come and gone here
Flooding and receding
Leaving shelved limestone
That our boot cleats bite and hold

We study the ceaseless hefting of water
For there is no other signature
Water rock two hunters and the fish:
Dark shapes deliberate in the shallows

Carp: as big as my son on his second birthday
Moving through this lake asking wordless questions
Picking things up and setting them down
A robust legendary fish

My first presentation fails: no turn
So I run the shore trailing coils of line
Waves watery gray and the steady black shapes
A good throw and the leader drops at perfect intercept

The moment set out before me: it comes to this
Count down strip hard fast then slower
With the false goby I demand the gaze of a carp
Our eyes meet and she peels away from the group

A pivot of ninety degrees into the line of retrieve
A giant tracking a fly: ten feet and still coming
I kill the streamer and she slows
A pulse of the mouth and there, she took it

Strip set and simultaneous lift of the rod
To a glorious bow pointing emphatically down and out
The carp runs that direction to endless miles of water
We look around at no one and wonder

What this all means isn't clear but that doesn't devalue it
One thing is true: this world is not wallpaper
There's a need to be in it and to connect
I exhale as line rips away
    Knowing this as a mode of worship

Spring burning

The Christmas tree
Is a conical pyre
Fierce such that my father
Presses his calloused hands
To the siding

Hot he says do you remember
When we burned the shed
Had to cut a hole in the ice
Bail water onto the house
I remember

The heat tends an invisible
Barrier we all step back
The pillar sways
Snaps at the boys
Who stare and reach

Next is the deer carcass
Meat left between ribs
Smolders and then lights
Like woven wafers
Of oiled wick spitting

The cells and tissues
Built at long labor
Here burst in varying light
The muscles that held antlers
In virility flame and blacken

We push the hind legs forward
Like kindling remnants
Next morning just ashen
Holes and fissures blacks grays
The skeletal made delicate

Outstate Minnesota winter

On a February day with no wind
The backdoor opened and closed
And his father walked into the kitchen
Heavy boots striking deep notes in wood

The man leaned forward palms on the table
Head bowed eyes up looking at the boy
Under one hand was a rough-hewn knife
Leather cord wrapped for a handle grip

All them hens have gotta go son
They're about dry and the ones that ain't
They've taken to eating their own eggs
Bunch of 'em in there all busted shells

The boy unmoved stared out the window
Where God's own sun struck the snow
Were waves of flashing pinhead diamonds
Tree shadows like dark currents cut through

He shifted focus to his father and said nothing
Studied his oil stained coat and frayed cuffs
The man pushed himself up from the table
Stood in quiet and then turned away

Gripping the knife over loud even steps
Toe to toe back the way he had come in
The boy watched him move through the yard
Through alternating light and shadow

Adviso

He never did give much straight out advice
But that night we sat the table late
His hands on a beer bottle
My eyes on his hands
Do your work and don't talk he said
The words came sidelong:
Just do your work
And don't talk a lot

Carcass

They all look like this
When the meat's off
Cows pigs deer all

The boy's hands are small
Just encircling the axe handle
He can use it only
In the fashion of a tamp

The ribs breaking before him
White and brittle
Having sat the weather some months

Rural

There are no houses anywhere
Never have been any I reply
Not in the history of the world
He peers out, reckoning that

Your mom and I found a train
Of snapping turtles here years ago
Just going from A to B was all
Big dragons pulling their bulks

We stopped to help them across
They gaped and craned and pawed
See it was objectionable to them
Even having a road—just a road

I remember the tails: scaled, studded
Gaping mouths hissing damn you
Damn it all this was an old path
An old way you cut through here

Winter

Deer came up the draw at night
Tracks where they'd jump the fence
To chew down the raspberry canes
He'd never heard of that before

Chickens stopped laying
All save the young leghorn
Red over white over reptilian legs
One egg maybe every other day

He screwed soup can stilts
Under the legs of the tree stand
So as to raise the angel higher
Atop the humble balsam

He augured holes in the pond ice
So the boy could jig for koi
The slow orange phosphorescence
Patterned in dark water

One night he vomited in the frozen garden
His wife brought a warm washcloth
Said she could hear him through the walls
Kneeling and retching in the snow

Li Bai

When I found this riverbank
The wine flask was full
Now it is empty

And so the pigeons
Stand in great contrast
To the vast humbling sky

People walk the path
I don't know them
They move with purpose
But I don't understand

Tree branches overhead
Dark angles and elbows rattling
In wind that cuts through my clothing

But it is like I tell my children:
There is no worry this close to home
Minutes from warmth

Four Short Drinking Poems

I. December Friday Night

I like setting an old
Broke-tipped knife
On a wooden shelf
In my garage
After shucking bark
From a buckthorn staff
And then dropping
An empty beer bottle
In a five gallon bucket

II. December Saturday Night

Who wants to drink
Plunk at the green keys
Of a Sterling typewriter
And maybe tie some flies
In the basement
I do

III. April Sunday Night

After two strong beers
Dosed to blur the ambient
Rip a bit on a guitar, then
Set a 14.5 inch dead trout
On a cutting board
Pour some whiskey
Turn on Muddy Waters
Go from there

IV. June Sunday Afternoon

Hey why wouldn't the newspaper man
Take my messages
I mean why wouldn't the mail man
See my photos
Shit I mean why's the flag still up
On the mail box
It's Sunday she says
Okay I say

Round trip to Dillingham

I. Man from Taboona

My grandfather was a Swede like yours
And my grandmother a native
Photo of a broad-faced beautiful woman
One of The Beach People

The cultures are similar
Oak stream hard water hard heads
Photo of a family processing meat
He is held in a long reminisce and I wait

When my uncle saw I was a hunter
He named me Sees the Moon
Or Sees What Others Do Not
And so I have killed seventy-five moose

He holds standing in two worlds
Careful dark eyes and thick crooked fingers
Pushing images on an iPad
He speaks to what is before him

But seems to stare through or past
It was one hundred miles to Anchorage
My father and I would take turns rowing
For two and a half days

He points to a sculpture: shaman hunting on thin ice
And here baying wolf with broken jaw
Creativity he says is uncovering what's inside
And knowing when to stop

We feel land come tight to the plane
Shake hands at parting and he says
Remember it's river rainbow you want
Lake rainbow tastes like mud

II. Man from Togiak

When I was a boy we had winter
We hunted on our snow machines
Twelve ptarmigans in my backpack
Or maybe two snowshoe hares

We would be gone for days
Big voices and little voices out there
Now people laugh at snow machines
There is no snow and there are no hunters

I like how you do that he says
How you say thanks for everything
I'm going to be better about that
He raises his foam coffee cup

Drinks with two rough-cut hands
And a wide-eyed reverence
His gaze everywhere intense
An old young man

Yup'ik: The Seal Oil People
The oil is magic and it burns in your mouth
My grandmother could skin a seal
Perfectly: taking all the fat

Some quiet and then: Togiak Village
I had to leave
Black peaks at the window
We finish our coffee in quiet

He pushes his napkin to the tray corner
Strokes it smooth then suddenly still
My grandmother he says without blinking
She used to save things like this

On Gull Lake

What is your starting point
Your basic premise here
They had some lee near shore
But it died with the shadow

Such that they came into light and wind
Together both pushing them
And the granules of snow sand
Moving in waves sorting in dunes

Walking west to east
Thinking about what they'd done
Talking intermittently
According to the voice of the northwest

When one turned to face the other
The howling in the ears ceased
Such was the tangent angle
You can find faults in all people

The far shore would not come
And they thought of others
Who had walked this ice path
They talked of others and kept on

At the tree line were dolphins
And great gray-backed serpents
Glistening breaking the snow waves
They rested and shared drink

If you look hard you will find faults
On the return trip they found drifts
Over their footprints were drifts
More elegant than the mark of any man

On Wind Lake

This pike's skull was smashed
A granite handstone, hours ago
Yet its gills flare under the knife
There is little doubt the fish sees me

At night my nose suddenly pours
And I find bleeding cuts on my hands
Air stills and a curtain falls over camp
Bringing the profoundest silence

This pike was the lake, never apart
An actual calcification from the water
When I kill it I dig under a canvas
For a buried dimension of primalism

Today's is not the world of the old days
But here we still cling to fire, ringed by dark
Wolves bay the moon just back of camp
Pacing the obscurity of balsam thickets

Words and hands of men mean little here
We bow quietly, eating billion-year old rock
Dissolved in water transmuted to flesh
To perceive this joinery is the tribute

Head shot circa 1987

Here is the axis deer
Raising its head to look
Dropping low browsing
A quivering and heavy hide

Raising lowering wary
Of us: all tensed and still
Silent watching the barrel
Studying the age spots

On his crooked forearm
Gun metal not gripped
Only resting long and grayed
And then a shot

An acute violence
We look to him, crouched
He rises slowly maybe mournfully
We wade into the meadow

The eyes had exploded outward
Hanging as if in some disbelief
We reach out to touch
Back boys back let him be

I grip a hind leg just above
Cloven hoof it kicks repeatedly
As if to repel us each and all
As if to say let me be

Sheep rancher

Every morning
I would put in a chew
Holster a thermos of coffee
And drive the pastures
Breaking ice in each trough

The dense wool
Sound and movement in pattern
A hundred breaths
Steaming in winter sun
All bowing at the water

Eighty-seven year old woman on abandoned building patio I.

Straight line winds came
Took shingles from the garage roof
And many trees
Even the copse of birch

But not the big white pine I replied
That was always our third base

It's beautiful and strong isn't it
I walked the grounds crying
And your brother said don't cry
Trees grow back

Well:
Some of those stumps
We counted on some of them
More than eighty rings

Eighty-seven year old woman on abandoned building patio II.

He called and said come over
You have to see what I shot
So we went over
Long drive you remember

It was two dogs he had killed
And we had seen those dogs and heard them
Coming through our ranch to his
Enormous shaggy creatures and one wearing a cowbell

So we knew the owners
Neighbors on the other side
But didn't say anything about it
They had gone too close to the kids he said

Later that night Marge owner came knocking
Asking after them saying they'd run off
We despised lying and dishonesty
But we didn't have the heart to tell her either

I can still see those big dogs and hear that bell
Other night I prayed and recalled a friend's name
If I pray tonight I will remember
The names of those dogs

Belle Creek

What about that parking lot
Just downstream of White Rock bridge
Do people still dump refrigerators
Water heaters whatever else there

Yeah they do
And there's another one
Just north of Vasa
Parking lot for some DNR land

One spring we got a call
Someone had dumped a horse
Just left her there entirely
Come spring she got to stinking

We had to take her out of there
Dig a hole with a backhoe
He said and looked down
A horse requires quite a hole in the ground

Watching the sunrise from a deerstand near Weaver Minnesota

This is as close as a man can get
To feeling the Earth move beneath him
That is my contention
As the land turns to the waiting sun

The tree in which I am perched
Has grown in response to its place
It leans from the sideslope dark limbs reaching
And it eats light which is a foundational miracle

In this valley where leaves go back to dirt
And one great river joins another
It is apparent: we cannot kill the world
We have only a hand in writing our own chapter

How to process black walnuts

First thing you do is resolve
that you will let Planet Earth
do most of the work for you.
To that end, you do not touch
a green walnut. Let them be.
Do not pluck them from the tree.
Don't think of forward, reverse
with your car in the driveway
playing at premature dehusker.
The wind, sun and rain will rot
for you the epidermis. Maggots
of the genus Rhagoletis will help
too. Do not look down your nose
at the writhing white forms.

When the nuts are brown, softening
in your grass, find your buckets.
Galvanized pails and plastic
five-gallons work well. Fill them.
Then let them be. The elements
and the maggots will continue work
for you. When you have some beer
handy, top the buckets with water.
Let everything steep for a while.
And now another resolution is made:
there is no tool. None but hands.
Plunge your own human hands into
the black blood of the black walnut.
Welcome the coffee stain to your skin.
It is your brand as taker of protein.

Search for the gimmes first: nuts
that have already shed their coats.
Throw these into another bucket.
Preferably a galvanized to afford
you a sequence of satisfying clinks.
Next feel for the husks that want
to come off; just need some coaxing.
Your hands are built for this job.
Clink, drink, clink, clink. Repeat.
Appreciate the black smudges and stains
on the bottle label. Maybe open another.
When your galvanized pail is heavy with
dehusked walnuts, fill it with water.
The next step is based on a slurry.
Enough water to make a walnut slurry.
Use your old shovel handle to whisk
the slurry into wild revolution.
The nuts will abrade one another, thereby
executing your secondary cleaning.
By their very nature and shape, they
will press and rub and remove the last
bits of their natal husks. Drain and
repeat. Stop when all is clean, clicking.

One night in a food dehydrator will do.
If you don't have one, employ a more
passive method, but maintain spacing.
The goal is to eliminate external moisture.
That night, while drying, think of
the black heartwood and the dripline.
Read a bit about allelopathy and the
exudate that dominates your soil and

now colors the lines of your hands.
Use a file to scrape the husk from
under your nails and wonder if maybe
you heard this one hit the shed roof
in the dark under the drooping canopy.
Next morning turn off the dehydrator.
Let them be for a bit, spaced out well.
Later on, about when you feel like it
put the nuts in burlap—coffee bean
sacks work well—and hang them
out of the way in your basement.

Let them cure until Christmas or later.
Reach your hand in now and then and
appreciate the dryness. Burlap dust
and the clicking. Take a bowl-full out,
touch each nut with your table vise. Find
the rest of the beer and finish the
shelling with a pair of snips. The cuts
you need to make will show themselves.
As the meats come free, fill a good
glass jar. The rate of extraction is
approximately half a cup per beer.

Netting suckers

We rose before dawn in cold dark spring
Drove forgotten two-track roads
Through forest canopy to dim corridors of water
To stand as brothers in pushing current
Landing nets held fast between our legs

Upstream Cousin poled fish forward
From the calm of their deep holds
From the silted pool bellies
They fled downstream riding hope
But there was only our waiting gauntlet

Suckers: the dark elongates
Dark like my memory of the stream
Cold darkness fluid and smooth
Came to our nets not apart from water
But as shadows born of it

From streambank to rough burlap sacks
From the forest to the back lawn
We used heavy dull knives
To make rough cuts along spines
The blood is in the grass that still grows

Splayed brined fish meat
Arranged in a block smokehouse
And a fire set to smolder
Our corporeal beings flesh and bone
Can be traced back

To swimming white suckers
That followed an old instruction
To run upstream with the lengthening day
Against the pushing current
Through wooded dark

Deer camp circa 1940

after looking at a family photograph

This is rough sawn lumber
A slant ceiling and somber walls
What is needed is here

Wood fueling fire warming air
Fire heating iron boiling water
This all for the men

Each in coarse wool wear
Resting on bare mattresses
Rising to clasp a shoulder

Holding simple metal cups
For there is no gadgetry here
Only a membership

They who have stared steady
Down steel into the heart
The warm beating heart

They who have knelt in the cold
With hands on the light of the forest
And watched it color the snow

Agulapak

From above the rivers
Are planar winding ribbons
Inset mirrors curving through
Ground few men have walked

Apparently two dimensional
Until the De Havilland Beaver
Touches the top of the weight
Of water

Some cold gray of the world
From which we climb over gunwales
Rods jointed all eyes alive
Set adrift

Our boat drafts and slides
We see inside now
Studying stones and seams
Men who live to read water

Fish are in good lays
Smooth muscular silver shapes
Piercing the three dimensional
We reach to hold them

At the far bank he leaves the boat
Standing in the Agulapak
He loved this river he says
And this would be a good place

At eye level the rivers
Are volumetric
Therefore they hold things
They keep substance

Like the ashes he releases
To the Immortal River:
It keeps our residues
Twisting in meltwater

In Falling Red Pines

Edna Lake circa 1994

The pike were taken from dark
Water, by men in a rowboat
There were no other people
No lights or buildings or roads

The fish were made hot over fire
We leaned in, a three-man circle
Our heads centering on the food
Grimed eager faces in the heat

Fingers reached into the pan
Arms embraced plates on laps
The act is indeed an embrace
Of that which will become you

Lapping and wolfing sounds
Nods and low mumbling content
No words
Only fire, water and meat

Only the free and flowing savages
Dark in the dark night, understanding
Neither what we had achieved
Nor what was to come

Sleeping in falling red pines

We are too far in to run out
The tempest has come
Sand does not hold roots well

We lay on our backs, listening
Outside dark, wind and rain
All bowing our walls inward

What will we do, you ask
If they start to fall
Where can we find cover

The goliaths wail and groan
Run to the lake, you say
Hide in the undercut bank

Waiting in a stranger's North Dakota home

He set various ammunition
On the dining room table
Told us about the day a tornado
Picked up his sister's house

Picked it up
Spun it around
Set it down
Quarter mile away

We nodded and fingered
Heavy stamped cartridges
Heavy brass and silver colors
Meant for taking things apart

And hell, the crows, too
They'd sweep in, big murders
Just savage the grain fields
We gassed 'em but EPA stopped us

Sun through windows
All slant dust motes
No one spoke
A few long ticks

The house sour, abandoned
Curse words piled in corners
Peeking out from behind
Fading family photographs

Floods too, we've been stricken
With any number of plagues
He sucked the thick atmosphere
Through his acrid cigarette

Ammunition of various shapes
Do you know what this is
Yeah, we know what this is
And we set them down

Heavy brass and silver colors
Loud on the cheap veneered table
They were heavy on his family table
And we walked out

Last fish

On a jutting rock
A big-ferruled rod
Doubled over hard
Line cutting s-curves
An ink-black catfish below

Decades of hefting
Two-eyed cement blocks
Pushing wheelbarrows
Corded his forearms
Broadened his back

He is a tapered man
Narrowing from the top
Like the catfish
That will not concede
They are coupled, pulling

He handles casually
A smiling dying man
Handling a departure
Ennobled by a last fish
Born of caliche and rain

He refuses my assistance
Touches his straw hat
Rests elbows on knees
Here is the final round
I squat at his side and watch

The catfish is joined by a twin
Shadowy illusory but yes
There are weaving s-curves
We stare in wonder
Staying connected

Hands coarse and heavy
Hands of countless miles
Now in recession
But they can still cup a fish
And hold a life with care

This one he considers gratefully
Bowing low to the water
Sliding the fish to its companion
We watch in the free air
As they tail off to their world

Driving to Decorah in late February

Fillmore County slides by at the window
Everywhere evidence of its layers:
Snow over soil over bedrock
Ancient ocean floors
There was saltwater here

The sun comes inside
I squint through it
Outside it is eating snow
There have been countless springs
And I know I'll never leave this place

We count nine hawks
Mostly big red-tails
Perched in majesty
Wind touching breast feathers
The oldest coats of arms

They watch from pinnacles
Not heeding roads or cars
Studying Earth's curvature
As the white rinds are
Peeled from their fields

Li Bai at the South Fork

A bright glass late summer moon
Rocks push the water up toward the light
The dragon-jawed spotted trout lays silent
In the sliding sheet below the riffle

I hold a length of cane over the water
Trailing a silk line and a feathered fly
It spreads a small v-wake in the current
Offering a connection between our worlds

In a sudden fury, the fish explodes at me
Hanging a deep bass note in the falling dark
As fireflies begin to rise at streamside
Like lanterns above villages of grass

Li Bai and Du Fu work upstream on the North Branch

They lingered in a quiet
That matched the color of the rock
Figuring about what to do
Just risen from drunken sleep
Sprawled on limestone bedworks
Two sot-gods with matted hair
Cracked and calloused feet
One clutching his arm
Scratching bramble wounds
The other pushing at coals
Tapping the flat rocks
With a charred spear
There were strewn about rib cages
Sharp pointed fish bones

Do we keep going up
His first words were framed
By a tribute of bowing nettles
Keep going up or call it
There are more corner holes

The other did not raise his eyes
This fire is like no other
Wood from all forests
No branches of the same tree
They crossed one hundred riffles
And delayed in swirling eddies
This is the river bend
They've been coming to forever

The embers collapsed further
Deep orange beset with black spackle
Pulsing bloodbeating portents
He rose and scanned the valley
Walls in which they were contained
Go on feeling small here
In this place of certain immensity
That's what I mean to do
They shouldered their packs
Kicked at the silent fire
And started upstream

Rain

Here, listen to me son
When the Earth's blood
Comes sheeting down

Or comes pounding
In heavenly droplets
Size of your thumbnail

You pay attention
Because one sure thing
It's not just weather

Take this compass plant
Got a turning head
It follows the sun

Been building a root
Over some decades
Probably ten feet deep

So this ain't a light matter
Look in the garden son
Every God-given green

Is exhalin' heavy now
And on the inhale
They're drinking the rain

Your sixth birthday

Bottom-right corner of the state
It's warm and fish are rising
We watch, resting on limestone
Sun and shadow have cut
A perfect diagonal
Across the bridge of your nose
I turn to you with a question

You do not answer
You cannot answer, I know
Even as the words meet air
Because you have found something

Reaching out into the light
You touch a strand of perfect silk
Suspending the last rain drop
From the morning's shower
It gathers the sun in a point
And wicks to your open hand

Fetching a pepper

Number 8 skillet is hot
Olive oil snapping, spitting
Under yellow stove light
Outside is October

Go out in the gray, son
Look for a bright red
Heart, hanging in a bush
Centered amongst green limbs

See the four chambers
What came of dirt, water and sun
Break apart the lobes
Start them to burn

The cold

Freezing can be tough
On a guy's operation
I've seen six glass milk jugs
Splintered to prisms
On the back step
Groaning beer cans
Pushing out their guts
In two directions
Eggs dying in their beds
Bursting along seams
Made visible only by the cold
Old Man Winter's
Cruel magic trick

Outstate Minnesota spring

His glove off to collect the eggs
Each covered in rank poultry foul
He lays them in the heavy snow

Following piss-colored boot waffles
Back to the garage service door
He pauses only to consider the frost

That he knows still reaches downward
And inward searching out his pipes
Beneath his feet and in his heart

A rhythmic dripping from the roof
Soft clucking of chickens in sun
And now a boy appears at the door

Don't go askin me for nothin son
Rolling the grimed eggs in his hand
Because nothin's about all that I got

Outstate Minnesota fall

Don't go out to the backyard
Father, after so many drinks
You're sure to cut yourself

Through cracked window pane
The deer swings, ghastly pendular
Heavy glass clicks the tabletop

Will you sew the holes in the hide
Well the holes are real holes
Son, there's no sewing them up

It's a long road with no exits
What you have won't be enough
So learn the value of sure things

Like light lying down to die
Heart and antler dying in sumac
Rising again at your family's table

Du Fu laments the changing landscape

As a boy I had asthma
The only remedy was to walk
Amongst waves of grass
With my father, shooting pheasants

The dog's black lips were gentle
Holding shimmering feathers
We all understood our places
In the world

When I was fifteen the old dog died
And all the grass was plowed under
Our hunting lands grew quiet
And forbidden

I left to climb jade mountains
Taking words from high clouds
My bare feet grew worn with
Wandering

Now home again, gray and drinking
My house abandoned to the croppers
I bow my head at the window
Lamenting

My asthma has returned, the grass has not
Fingers of wine cling to green glass
And everywhere the tink tink
Of corn grains filling the coffers

John Bass

After casting from high rock walls at Cruising Fish

In one of the last bars in the Midwest
John Bass sat a wooden stool
And to the man next to him:
If there were money I'd buy you dinner
I appreciate you takin me out

The local was smoking hard
Hands well-grimed pinching the rolled cigarette
His frame compact and very dense
He appeared to be coiled
Perhaps from accumulating rage

But they were on good terms
Now drinking together
Waiting on whatever food could be offered
The local set a glass down heavy
Stared at it

I got ticks on me today
Walkin in grass that ain't been walked
By anybody but me for decades
How the hell you figure that's possible
There was a barmaid and she looked up

How can they be so thick year after year
Bass drank said nothing
You know they sit on a grass blade
Front legs out just waitin
They sit on a grass blade and wait

They stared at empty glasses
I don't know how they do it
The local got up and walked around the bar
Uncorked an opaque bottle:
Waitin out prey like that

Bass nudged his glass and looked at the man
Face forward he showed close-set eyes
His father always said
The mark of a criminal
Whatever the case appreciate you taking me out

You've got some good water there
Glasses now full and quiet
Only sharp metallic punctuations from the kitchen
Where the hell you get all this liquor
Well we got ways to get it

Even today we got ways
They studied old twisted neon lightworks
A script gone dull
The mirrors cracked and pieces long vanished
This all susceptible

Only the dense wooden bar had endured
Only the heavy plank
With some lingering resemblance to a God-given origin
Bass fingered the grain
Subtly topographic

The sun had set well
And in the gray interior the men were framed
Disjointedly by the cracked wall mirror
Some geometry of resignation in which they reflected
Headless faceless waiting

John Bass removes a stump

What he liked most
Stopping to study his actual body
Leaning on the pommel of the axe handle
The hair on his arms matted
S curves crossed under by dark veins
Of good dirt

Most of which was gone now
And so he especially loved these heavy sweats
The world was more dimensional
The skyline a greater contrast
All movements were understood
Felt through genuine sweat

About half the wood gone
He began crying out at the arc
Each swing burying the head
The pattern he cut was perpendicular
Lines in pattern to free wood
He yelled and sweated

The dense tree heart
Chunked and flew at him
And a woman walked by with her daughter
Without speaking he said I am a man
Soaked through with sweat
Stopping to wave

Then sitting with axe across his knees
Wondering on the best he could do in this age
When most is stripped away
He drank and watched the rain come
Slowly and completely with abstract stamps
Overtake the smoothworn axe handle

Bass remembers his father in camp

He told me once his favorite morning
Was watching the April sun come up
Come up over the east valley wall
And glint on his coffee workings

After pouring a cup he'd rest the pot
At the edge of the coal bed handle out
And keep at tending the cook fire
Doubling it over folding it inward

Nudge each stick along carefully
These little fires they're fragile matters
I think he figured for the most part
People didn't tend to much anymore

Without a word he'd throw coffee dregs
We'd cruise for more dry hung deadfall
Come back armloads and dragging branches
Just sit and watch wood come apart

The earliest memory of John Bass

These ice sculptures run a thousand bucks apiece
Look at this one here like a big goose of sorts
They passed beer cans from one hand to the other
A cold black night above but here on earth

Blinking lights and the last chapter of socialization
An arquebus is just an old gun you mean a hook gun
They said and said more the cans always moving
The eyes of the goose were bright points of light

Like a devil goose and I pressed my mitten to it
I remember the mitten on the goose when he came
From the side shadow from the darker perimeter
And he pushed his voice out leaning painfully

My mother she is sick and I worked all day
His lips moved as if yelling but each word was muted
To get money I need an ambulance for her please
And each please ended with a ticking wheeze

I saw people moving but they were all one
The music and the people were a great flowage
Within which we held a border for our pocket
Into which this stranger had come gesturing pleading

He concluded his address and the men stared
I hung my hand on the bill of the goose and looked up
Dark geometry of abandoned buildings framed by stars
His eyes were sad and supplicating and he ever leaning

We don't have any money said my father
In the alternating blue and red lights I saw his eyes
Shift downward as he lifted a beer can
The man said thanks guys and he shuffled away

John Bass rides into the site formerly called Wykoff

They sat together stoics
Clenching and relaxing fists
Weathered knuckles
On a hardwood table

Each watching the other
Murmuring sometimes speaking
The room heavy with salt and smoke
And they of salt

Their common clothing
Enduring canvas and wool
Grimed heavy at the cuffs
All grays browns worn well

Look it's been a good year
He fingered grooves in the table
Some with the grain some cut across
Another year passed in quiet

They pointed and studied
Yellowed papers blacked letters
What is our path here
The words all typed neatly

A good year a new measure
We could get used to this yes
Eyes turned down again
Back to the crackling paper

Some loose piles some pinned
And what do you do now mostly
Concern myself with the day's course
Put up wood get food

They said it would be violent
And what is it you do now
Do you look in on deer bones
Cached in deep glens

What I do mostly is study
Fish smoke and wash my feet
Outside quiet was draped on all
A long-standing return

There were sheathed roots
Ever-burrowing in dark
And inside burning wood
What can you say John Bass

They did say it would end in fire
And indeed rodents now drag bellies
But not through blooded soil
Some saw it not all I think you did

John Bass we have been afforded this
A heavy hand on the tiller
Here is more split wood
Dry to warm us

His thumb again touched a volume
Embossed with a red-tail whispering
When the cities lie at the monster's feet
There are left the mountains [1]

[1] Lines from Robinson Jeffers

The grackles came to the quarry edge

From the cornfield just south
They settled as a great wind
Pushing and turning air currents
Beset with darkness
An audible lighting
On oaks and poplar
On the wirecolored cottonwood
In which he was posted

At these sudden dark perches
He stared in wonder
Gradients iridescent: blues blacks
Each twitching head
A discerning monocular
In some panel of gloom
Each jerking turn a syllable
I have shared smoke with the devil

Others have come they said
And they have quit this land
They are right about you
Much work remains
And they lifted as one dark form
Branches light with relief
The black chant receding
Gone off to the north

His uncles taught him to throw the spear

Long ice saws
They fold out like jackknives
You can see here yourself

Just metal on ice
Metal on flesh
I see that you see

Granules of snow
Falling into still water
And the perfect clarity

In the dark of the house
You aim for the head
The seeing eyes of the spearshaped fish

In that way you get the best
Of Him: old esox lucifer
He sees the justice in it

As the spear moves he feels
Water moving but the justice
That it's his own likeness killing him

Take the trident son
Lean close and watch
Stand guard piscator and venator

He dreamed an alternate death for his grandfather

He left the truck on high ground
Walked around the shack down to the tank
Found him laying flat out on the caliche
Straw hat over his eyes just resting

Next thing he saw was the neighbor's dog
Salt and pepper mutt with a long wagging tongue
Not a tongue: a banded snake, half-eaten
What in the hell and he ran for a shovel

Is that a bunch of damn snakes he yelled
Yes and an ivory serpent started forward
Moved slowly to the silent laying figure
Drew back, head flaring flat with menace

Here the boy hesitated one breath only
Not wanting to strike his grandfather with the blade
And in that time the snake bit the man
Set on his face with two bared fangs

Did he bite you he kept screaming
Yeah he did, the older man said, calm
Who lays on the ground in this country anyway
I should have hit him first thing

But I was afraid he said and they sat together
Wailing and lamenting their if-onlys
And then the boy chopped through scales
Leaving the snakes in silent writhing pieces

West southwest wind recedes

How wind could touch one ground
With such severe focus
Was not known to him
The whirling devil of chaff
Streaming across the field
Drab husks and leaves in pattern
Conical maybe helical
Twisting through some signature
Of the southwest wind

When it ever-pressed like this
The ears were useless:
He did slow turning scans watching
Through elbows of gray branches
All limbs in undulating waves
Swaying fore and aft in time
With his own perch

Around dusk it finally gave out
In a sort of concession
Leaving an abrupt settling in its wake
A silence that gained weight quickly
Within which he became aware
Of a regular moaning
Rising from the draw across the field
From the land's deep cut
Some anguished cry rising falling
From the jointed limestone walls
Up through the spidered wreckage
Rusted twisted iron castoffs
Up across the field's humping shoulder to his tree

It did not quiet as night came
And when he lay on the ground
Some hundred yards from the stand
He set a heavy knife in his boot
Pommel up
And watched leaves falling in dark
Then stars through woven canopy
Various dream states and night sounds
Complete depth of sleep never achieved
The way of all hunters he knew

He rose in the still-dark first morning
From some middling drowse
Forms and words in his mind
As real as any grass blade or tree trunk
There before him now

He dressed in silence
Retraced his steps
Back toward the field edge
Rhythmic moaning growing louder
He paused at the tree and listened
Some painful call or plea
Some fact embodied in real flesh
That he would never see nor understand
He climbed the ladder and made still
Waiting for the sun in the eastern sky

Tying a Smallmouth bass streamer fly

Black wool shorn on Prairie Creek same day it was passed to me we were given a frozen humanoid shape with no hands or feet or head frozen and curled it had been stroked when it was soft and mammalian and it had been cared for and smiled upon then killed too with great care and split longitudinally and skinned a heavy knife cut off the head and the extremities and I suppose blood ran into the ground we roasted a five meridianed rabbit and the black sheep that grazed near this rabbit gave its very hair to have it wait eleven years in my possession to be tied onto a streamer hook wrapping and blinding the drab eyes and from here with the rabbit built in me and the wool in a black suitcase we will paddle north and east in the line of the ice gougings and then lay our tack and equipment out with noble purposes including reaffirming gender looking at raptors smelling various elementals and plant tissues patting one another on infrequently touched shoulders and moving canoes on top of the weight of water which holds meat that can be consumed by man this fly will be selected and assigned and it will fall directly down it will push its woolen head into the lakebed and then by way of a series of careful bunchings it will bounce up and with the first bounce it will plume silt then it will make a pattern of obtuse peaks and valleys working in a line back toward me the maker there will be apex predators in the vicinity and by some poorly understood code they will fin toward the fly's path and charge it again and again they will drive with caudal fins they will backferry using pectoral fins in moments of indecision one though will be unable to resist and it will rise up from the gray in a helical pattern and in one actual action it will open and flare and the wool will disappear within it.

Gar

Cloutier found Bass in his lower deck cabin unlacing his boots. Both men were bleached and wind-worn having returned from a day on the big water adjacent to the Gulf. Bass looked up but Cloutier said nothing; he seemed to be just waiting. Bass said that he had been thinking for a long time about a shot of tequila. He didn't do that sort of thing all that often but he said he'd been thinking about it most of the afternoon and he'd decided he was going to do it. Maybe several shots with some of the salt and lime wedge in the captain's bar upstairs. Cloutier approved of the idea but declined to take part himself. He turned in the doorway to leave but Bass stopped him: I wish the gar had raked my face, he said. I wish he'd raked my face when he thrashed his way out of the boat this morning. Cloutier studied his partner but did not speak. Maybe three or four lines across here Bass said and pointed to his right cheek. A mark of permanence. Bass looked up at Cloutier who nodded in understanding and then left for the boat deck.

Brown trout

The river flowed toward him, over the rocks and around his calves. John Bass crouched and let one knee touch the water. He stared down into it and saw a piece of flat limestone shaped like a bell. He reached a cupped hand into the river just above the bell and scooped water up and onto his neck. The coolness washed away the heat. He scooped more and wet his face and then went all out, dipping his hat into the water and pouring the bucketful over his head. Cold water ran down his back and even past his beltline into his pants. He looked upstream as a trickle crossed his temple and he saw nettles reaching down the bank toward the river and one conifer with its roots hanging out into the water like an empty cage. Mostly though he looked at the water and the way the light caught on the bumps pushed up by the rocks. There were rocks under these contours, and bugs of various sorts under the rocks. He knew that the bugs in those rocks struggled in their sheaths, pushing toward the adult mayflies that hung on the tall grass at streamside. Metamorphosing to the tan and black mayflies that clung to his clothes. Somewhat like the hackled fly he held between his left thumb and forefinger. He pinched the abdomen of the fly and studied it. The tail was still intact, although the fibers were brittle and some were broken off short. The body of the fly was gray and the wings were black and white. The reddish hackle extended to the tips of the wings. He blew on the fly and then shook it off. Adams.

Bass scanned ahead again, focusing on the broken water and the light over the riffle. Bugs hovering and bouncing. Occasional snips and slashes indicating rising trout. Bass let the fly hang in front of him, out of the water, while he stripped line from the reel. When a good pile floated around him he began false casting at a careful angle to avoid alerting the fish ahead of him. There were no steady risers. He searched the water from right to left, placing his fly in among the pockets, watching it with intensity as it floated back toward him. He was careful to strip line and mend to keep the fly floating high and without drag. His fly was bigger than most of the bugs around, and it floated higher than anything else on the water. He picked up a trailing drift and threw it to the head of a narrow aperture of slate gray water. His Adams floated over a submerged rock and slowed in the small eddy behind it. He watched a trout head break the surface then disappear. He picked up the rod and felt the resistance moving from side to side. He held steady and did not hurry. Too much pressure could pop a hook out no matter how big or small the fish at hand. He metered the line while keeping the rod at a good angle, stripping the line shorter and shorter as the trout shot from left to right and back again. When it was at his feet he pinched the line tight to the rod and knelt to scoop the fish with his left hand. A brown trout of average size with many small spots, none of which were well-defined. He looked into the right eye of the fish. He drew a heavy knife from his pocket and turned the trout slightly so the top of its head was facing up at him. He raised the still-folded knife and then swung it down to crush the skull of the fish. At the fourth hard strike the eyes of the trout bulged and its tail quaked to stillness. Bass flipped the knife open and pushed the tip into the belly. He cut from gills to anus and then used the tip to free the gills from the head. He pulled everything loose as one and then with the back of his thumbnail he pushed the dark longitudinal kidney out of its membrane. Rinsing in the current the fish trailed some dark red downstream. Bass watched the blood plume in the water. The fish was an outgrowth of the river and the rock. The blood came from there and it goes back there. He remembered the way his father spoke these words without moving his lips; how he would meet a gaze and then look away in conclusion. Bass folded the fish into his clothes and walked on.

The riffle extended to a curve in the river, which was the limit of his vision. To his left woody shrubs and small trees grew at the base of a towering cliff that defined the river's bank. Their roots clung to the very deepest of the rock's veins. To the right, a broad cobble bar, all flat limestone, sloped gradually upward to a grass bank. He felt the pull of his billowing pant legs as he eased upstream, working his fly across the riffle. Near the left bank, a trout rose three times but on each occasion refused the fly. Bass grinned intensely as he watched the fish move up from its lay, consider the offering and then turn quickly to retreat. This was how things worked: only some fish were to be taken.

By the time he got to the bend, he had captured two more trout, one of which he killed. The other was very small and the Adams dry fly had looked comically large extending from its lower lip. He released that fish and watched it push away to the rocks. Standing now at the bend, he looked upstream to his right at more riffle coming down from a slick. He sloshed over to the bank. His feet and legs tingled as he sat down in the grass of the first bench. All around him mayflies clung to pale green grass. He stared hard at one and then pinched its wings together and pulled it toward his face. The mayfly's legs pumped forward and back as it tried to grasp. The abdomen moved up and down as he set the fly back on a stem. It clutched the perch and immediately became still.

Bass was used to mayflies at this time of year but he still marveled at them. There was no getting over marveling at them. He pushed himself up with his left hand and brushed grass dust from his forearms. He picked up his rod and started upstream. Parting the blade forest, he kicked up a cloud of mayflies in front of him. He glanced behind and noticed how quickly the bugs settled back to the grass. Only a few flew out over the water. He moved up a little higher into the floodplain and walked under the walnut trees. They were old and big trees. Trunks so great a man could not wrap his arms around one. Bass stared out at the slick just above the riffle.

Everywhere dimple-rises drew larger and larger circles on the water before being overtaken by new dimples.

He walked away from the river across the limestone cobble bar and up the little shelf that marked the start of the walnut grove and its tall grass understory. Evening was just coming on and not much direct sunlight penetrated the canopy. The air had a calmness and grayness about it. There were mayflies even in the grove, up away from the river, and they rose from the grass in silence. Bass sat down with his back to a tree and looked at the water. He stared at the gear he'd left in a loose pile, at his rod leaning on one of the packs. He flaked away dried blood from the back of his left hand and looked down at the ground between his knees.

John Bass at Weaver Minnesota

A deer materialized down the draw and Bass sat the stand watching. It had come from somewhere but not anywhere that Bass understood and therefore to him it had come from nowhere. Some deer pushed sound ahead of them and others did not. Ground cover moisture and wind all mattered in this respect. When he was young Bass liked to think he could hear any deer well in advance of seeing it. He would go so far as to read on the stand for hours relying on his ears. By now he knew better though and indeed this deer had come in silence. It was lingering down at the edge of his sight where the day previous he'd watched two does for a good ten minutes. They had not afforded any sort of clear shot and after some time they seemed to disappear without actually leaving. When he had eventually shifted position in the stand they jumped from behind a copse of trees and fled up and away along the far slope. Now this deer was taking shape in the morning grayness. Picking along the draw, which was the defining feature of the small landscape within which man and deer now breathed and watched. One still and the other moving slowly along the sloping shoulder of land, through the oranges and grays of leaf litter.

Bass predicted that the deer would angle up and away from him on the far side. But it kept on. He had scouted the points of crossing the gully and had trimmed one lane according to the best land bridge. A point of advantage. Bass waited without moving but lost the deer behind a tight group of trees. Despite the hunter hearing nothing the deer appeared again now closer. It was headed for a shooting lane and Bass resolved that if it came through he would shoot. He waited for an obstruction in the deer's line of sight to him and slowly raised the gun to his shoulder. He was successful in gaining the shooting position and he exhaled and was grateful for he knew that no movement was ever granted as safe and passable. Each of these small decisions and actions being pieces of what in sum might constitute a successful hunt.

On approaching the lane the deer changed pace such that it put forward a small burst and Bass did not shoot. He had a history of not shooting. Each man was built with some degree of decisiveness in him and there was a gradation to this attribute that was obvious to anyone in the world. For Bass at that time and place he did not have enough and so the deer walked on for there had been no shot. The deer continued up the draw and Bass held the gun in silence and stillness. At the land bridge over the gully it did indeed cross toward him and was clearly visible in the lane he had trimmed but there was no broadside or decent quartering angle. Just the working front legs and the occasional sound of leaves moved by hooves and the head-on approach of the deer now looking side to side in apparent complete security and confidence.

Bass repeated words in his head and he remembered his father saying that at some point you just have to shoot. Studying cannot go on forever. Remember the boxes. Shooting them at great distance and wondering about the hits. Walking to them to find they were all hits and marveling at the accuracy of a shotgun which feels in hand and in use like such an obtuse creation. You can punch shots through brush. The open sights will work. Look down the barrel. The deer walked directly toward his tree and then turned ninety degrees now moving up the near side of the draw following the gully edge. It curved toward the best shooting lane and the last one available to Bass who pivoted slowly in his seat. This time the deer did not jump through the lane rather it stopped completely and turned to look at the hunter. Or maybe just toward the hunter who did not need to move at all other than to squeeze the trigger. Bass was sighted tight behind the front right shoulder and he shot. An act that given the tool employed could never be completed with absolute confidence. Here is a metal apparatus that strikes to explode powder in a closed shell which pushes forward a slug of lead. The attached barrel guides this force and projectile in the pointed direction and the precision depends on the eye of a human placing a small metal bead in the right position considering both the horizontal and vertical. If executed well the projectile will punch a round hole in the animal doing great bodily damage impacting and tearing tissues. What can be done is regular shooting such that the gun is known and the various ammunitions are known. And then from this platform of familiarity look down the barrel and summon the best shot. Bass did as much and the deer jumped forward seemingly at the sound but more likely he figured at the impact. Jumped forward and paused. Turned to look and then jumped forward again before running up to the top of the ridge and stopping at the row of pines. Bass swiveled and ejected a shell and shot again. The buck disappeared into the conifers. He waited for a good time and then climbed down the oak tree. He had given explicit instructions to his hunting mates that they not come to his aid in any case. Bass generally did not care to bother others and he did not want to take time from their own hunts. But they disregarded his instructions and came to his stand to help him recreate the scene and events.

From what you are telling me it sounds like you missed him said one man. The hell I missed him Bass said and his mind went to the shooting of the boxes and he stated flatly that he had hit the deer. Okay where did you last see the deer asked the other who then took charge and executed a careful cutting process looking for the first sign. Only a few minutes passed. You hit him good he said.

They stood the three of them inside the tight corridor of pines. All looking down. The deer had not crossed through immediately but had run within the row for fifty yards. A red pine bough lay on the ground and it showed blood draped over fascicles and patterned in splotches on the bed of auburn needles below. The blood mixed with thicker tissue making strings of bright red. Outside the pines on the far slope they saw where the deer had pushed through tall grass heading down toward a band of sumac. Bass hoped it had stopped there because beyond the sumac a steep drop down led to the next valley over. They found blood on grass and on goldenrod leaves. Deep crimson markings. There was little question the buck had gone to its death. The tracker led the way but it wasn't long and Bass could see up ahead of him the place in the sumac. The two men stopped and Bass walked past them. The buck's mouth was bloodied but otherwise it looked like he had just laid down and died. There had been no thrashing or broken limbs and all the violence was hidden from view in the chest cavity behind the hole that Bass had caused there just back of where he'd set the bead. Bass knelt in the grass and unsheathed his knife. He looked up. Thanks boys he said and his mates left out for their stands.

Disappointment Lake

That year there were forest fires. Great billows of white smoke overhead in place of clouds; a constant eye-stinging haze over the water. The fire was burning around Pagami Creek and a passing fisherman had said that it wouldn't be out any time soon. On the fourth night camped on Disappointment Lake they heard noises at the water's edge. Cloutier walked to the beached canoes, searching smoke low over the water with a small point of light. A hollow sound like the beating of an empty drum led the beam between two canoes to the mossed shellback of a great turtle. The smoke and light together played on it gave the shell a mystical appearance: some beast come from gray depths attended by motes in air and in aqua. It's gleaming yellow eyes close-set and its carapace an old cross-hatch, plated and grooved and scarred. A water beast born of the very lake-stone and run over and worn down by decades passing. The turtle moved its head slowly in calculation and a bass on a stringer ferried backward and forward in fear, striking the canoes in a roughly-timed rhythm. Counting down its demise the man thought. He called the others to the spectacle and they all came down to shore.

That a creature so barnacled and obtuse of body could move with such burst fascinated the men. After three lunges the great beak held the bass, flattening its head unnaturally. From this point of advantage the turtle brought forward one foreleg at a time and situated it to maximize the tearing and ripping pressure. Beak and claw rendered the fish into strips of white flesh. All the while the flashlight beams played through smoke and water, reflecting in the eyes of the mythological. Later at the fire the group reckoned that the turtle was older than any man present. Cloutier thought of the quiet lakebed and the accumulated silt where all turtles sleep out the cold. He wondered at the turtle's discernment that brought it to the bass on the stringer.

In the morning the first man awake walked to the canoes. The stringer hung empty in the water and there was no remnant of the fish. It had vanished with the turtle and the man thought it was if it were never there.

Rainbow trout

Around camp Bass and his partners had established themselves as sticks and they were treated accordingly by the guides. No one talked to them about gear or technique or how to fish the rivers or how to fight salmon or rainbows or char. Mostly the guides just defined the general approach for each day and then navigated to the good water. On this morning though one of the guides asked Bass for his reel. Bass gave it over and the guide set the drag with great attention and iterative test strippings. Now don't touch it, he warned as Bass screwed the reel tight to the rod. The guide went further and told the anglers that they should do just as he would indicate. When fighting fish the rod tip should be kept up high at all times. Bass and Cloutier nodded through this series of preparations and headed for the dock.

There were a handful of fly patterns around the boat but they used only one: a flesh colored rabbit strip with the hook set well back toward the tail. The approach was to haul line and make big casts at approximately forty-five degree angles to the boat, then swing the fly down with the current. The guide kept to the oars and studied very carefully all of their actions. He watched the rod tips for any indication of a strike.

Bass usually had the look of a silent killer. He had even been so-named by some of the guides. When he felt the first fish strike he kept his cool as if he had expected it all along. The guide had been watching the rod tip and the line. He yelled at Bass to set the hook even as the angler came clear with a tight line and a bowed rod. Bass instinctively reached to palm the reel but the guide yelled very sharply at him: Don't touch the reel. The drag had been set to do the work and the whole business of current and fragile mouths, strong fish and pointed runs meant that the task of optimizing resistance during the fight should be left to the reel.

The fight did not last long. The fish leapt clear of the water. When the anglers exclaimed at the sight the guide turned in his seat to see for himself. The rainbow appeared as a giant bright football rising from the river. It seemed to peak at no less than six feet above the water. The trout reflected the sun, shining chrome, its great head shaking. Wide and long and very heavy it fell back to the river in a spectacle, leaving the line slack. The men discussed possible errors or misplays but all agreed Bass had made none. The guide confirmed that the fish was probably the Lone Pine Bow: a trout well-known around camp. Sometimes fish beat you. They can beat fisherman with long histories on rivers and streams and waters of the world. That the fish should win sometimes was just. This was not something the anglers said to comfort one another. It was truth to them. Without that truth the entire affair and thus their lives and relationships would be greatly reduced.

Bass hooked the next fish in a similar manner with the guide scolding him to keep the rod tip up. It was more of a reminder than a correction. Bass was very focused and the rod tip was high. Within seconds the fly line was gone and backing burned off the reel. The boat was near a falls, the roaring edge of their immediate world. The current in the slick felt very heavy. The outlook was not good. Bass said as much, studying the line going out and away from the boat: There's so much line out he muttered. Bass had fought many big fish of various species but he'd never had a trout take his fly line and half of his backing. It looks like he's headed for the falls, he said, and indeed the fish carried on downstream. The line seemed to go into the water at the top of the falls. Bass lost heart at this development. He was sure the fish was gone: No chance now. Don't worry, the guide reassured him. That fish doesn't want to be caught up in those falls any more than we do.

After some time the rainbow began swimming back upstream. Bass didn't know if it was because of the pressure of the heavy bowing line pulling on the lodged hook or the distress of holding in the rapids at the head of the falls. Maybe the combined forces were too much. Bass took line as he was able and soon he had his fly line back. He had come out of it okay. He was starting to think he would land the fish.

During the course of the fight the guide maneuvered the boat to shore where Bass, standing firm in calf-deep water, brought the fish to hand. The trout's back was gray-green, the bottom half of its body white run through by a swath of pink that intensified toward the tail. It was uniformly flecked with black, the tail nearly covered in spots aligned along the fin rays. Its eyes showed golden rings inset with large black pupils. A beauty inimitable. When Bass released the trout the anglers stood in admiration. Cloutier remarked on the width of its shoulders. It's not the Lone Pine Bow but it's a good one, said the guide. Let's go hook another.

Snowbank Lake trail

From the highest point they studied Flash Lake: calm on the leeside, small ripples windward that made the water look darker and textured. On the far shore a pattern of gold and brown and green with white pine standing a rank at the limit of their sight like a back-guard. White pine grew unpredictably in asymmetric branch patterns, while the red pine always grew like pipe cleaners. White pine look soft while the reds look bristly. Bass recalled this instruction from long ago but did not mention it. His companion pointed to a long bar of rushes reaching out into the lake to encircle a pool of sorts where three gray deadheads listed. At the end of the bar a treed rock island was floored with auburn needles. They agreed that the neck of rushes and the point looked hospitable for both fish and waterfowl. Both men made quiet remarks about the view of the lake and the surrounding forest. This was country unspoiled. Country left by the last age of ice. It had thereafter endured only footpaths and paddles from the world of men.

Backtracking on the portage trail they found an old rowboat stashed behind some conifers. Bit of a haul to get it back here, Bass said. He searched but found no oars under the boat. The men studied old, peeling registration stickers. Bass thought about the years printed there; wondered who had last put a hand on the boat. They continued on the portage trail to the intersection with the Snowbank Lake

Trail. There they left the portage, turning northeast to follow the lake's shoreline.

Bass carried an old shotgun, a simple device with a break action that took one shell at a time. On the sideplate the gun-maker had engraved a dog pointing in grass. Next to the dog were stamped the words Savage Arms Corporation, Chicopee Falls, Mass. U.S.A. The gun's dense metal and wood felt good carried in one hand, leaving the other free to navigate cross-branches over the trail or downed logs. They walked a long way, Bass twenty paces ahead of his companion, the sun touching both men. They stopped occasionally to study the country or pick wintergreen, which they chewed and stashed in their bottom lips in the fashion of tobacco. Much of the trail followed high rock and they could see Snowbank Lake. Flat and blue-gray. Bass sorted out in his mind how the lake and the rock underfoot and the gun in hand and the small oaks with leaves gone red and the towering white pines made him feel right. Clean and cool and prepared and alert in a good place. Boots holding well to whatever ground. This was all very pleasing and Bass thought about saying as much but did not because he knew it was unnecessary.

They descended into a little cut, crossed the tea-colored tributary stream; up the other side they walked into an old campsite. The black fire grate said in raised letters US Forest Service. No one had been there for years and the rocks around the grate had come apart, leaving it partially exposed. Three

big red pines had blown down. Their root bases still held soil and stone, all set in one direction like a series of ramparts. The men looked around and praised the
site for its good location.

They returned the way they had come, heading for their canoe. Maybe we'll see a grouse on the way back one said. Maybe said the other and they took to the path.

Muskellunge

The man took the seat just left of Bass. May I, he said, but it wasn't a question. Bass looked away and then at the man: he was dressed in a plain dark shirt with a rigid collar and buttons down the front, in the fashion of an officer. His face was well built save for a missing eye, and his expression was flat in a sort of matter-of-fact projection that seemed to fit the interior of the dim and quiet room. Bass thought it a good setting for meeting a one-eyed stranger. He actually thought that sentence, but all he said aloud was, Sure.

They made some small talk and a few minutes into the conversation the subject turned to fishing: You know the place just south where all the muskies are piled up.

I do know it, replied Bass.

When we were kids we used to run up and down that river. The muskies just stacked in the tailwater. No one really knew how many. A dozen or a hundred. Or more. In a few hours of fishing we would move two or three, hook one or two and maybe land one.

This day, the man said and pointed to his puckered eye socket, I was fishing alone, casting an old wooden lure. Three treble hooks. A big nasty painted stick, really. Meant for heaving and mechanically retrieving what was essentially a battleship of barbed points. I hooked the first fish I moved, and after just a few minutes a muskie of exactly fifty-one inches lay at my feet in the shallows. I was able to get about half of it in my net. We don't have nets specific to every occasion do we. As you know. So this particular net was undersized given the task at hand. I knelt low to the limestone and got my right hand on the fish's tail. I backed it out of the net and got the head clear. At its sudden freedom the fish bucked against my touch, launching against my face. One of those treble hooks, those big mean bastard hooks, one of them pierced my right eye. Barb pushed through.

The man paused. Bass looked at him and then down at his own hands. You can imagine what happened next, the story-teller continued, with that barb holding. You can imagine but I'll tell you anyway because it may be in the telling that I get free of it. Before I could physically react the weight of the fish pulled my eye from its socket. I groped about and dropped to the ground, following the fish that tore at my face. The eyeball was still attached to my optic nerve, so I could see through thick glass the face and eye of that muskie. It thrashed wildly and I pressed against it, calling out. Stuttering. The fish would go still and then build to writhing. My hands couldn't manage the living fish and the dangling eye on a barbed hook. I had to resist the urge to pull away. Finally I just bear-hugged the fish and squeezed with everything I had. I raised a stone and began striking the dragon-head.

Each blow of the rock brought a ringing pain to all my senses, but I kept on, trying to pin the fish down with my face while I bludgeoned at it. I could hear and feel the head breaking. But it was coming apart far too slowly, twitching through its expiration. I remember my ragged eye actually seeing with some clarity fish scales as the body finally stilled.

Of course I then had to remove a hook from my own eye. This I couldn't do. Nor could I take the lure from the fish's mouth. Too many variables and too much pain. I don't know if I thought the eye could be saved, or if I was just too afraid to tear it from my face. I walked home in alternating fits of silence and wailing, my eyeball bound to the mouth of the now-limp fish. My father assessed immediately that the eye was lost. He cut through what he called the cordage and worked that night to clean and cauterize. We left the bloodied fish out on the porch floor. Lure in mouth and my own eye speared there
hanging from the jaw of a muskie.

The man had leaned in close to Bass and said, I had you as a man who might relate.

Yeah, Bass replied. I'm that.

Seven pointer

Bass didn't hear the buck coming. It just appeared. Walking from west to east up above him along the wood edge. The deer was moving slowly lowering its head at intervals to inspect scrapes and rubbed saplings. It was focused and apparently cautious but unaware of the immediate presence of man. Bass raised his shotgun when the deer's head was behind a large tree. When it moved forward such that he could see just rear of the front shoulder he fired. He had decided to fire despite the shot being less than ideal: crossed by branches and thick bramble. He had confidence in the terrible weapon and he pointed it where it needed to be and pulled the trigger. The buck surged forward and turned a near-ninety-degree angle running downhill. Bass predicted his path and swung the gun around to his right. He had good lanes here and the deer did just as he'd figured and he even remembered in that moment his father saying that injured animals don't go uphill. When the deer came into the best lane he was running pretty hard and Bass tracked him with the barrel and fired. This time the deer collapsed and plowed through leaf litter, coming to rest on the gully edge, its body stopped by a small tree.

Later Bass would learn that the first shot was good but a little low and the second shot was high and that slug had shattered the deer's spine very near the middle of its length. He would touch the wrecked articulated chambers and the bone shards and the dark bruised strap meat. Even wonder at what he took to be the nerve fibers that had been a woven cord; that had moved consciousness. Synapses and some form of electricity at work linking sensory perception to reaction and movement and some unknown degree of thought.

Bass sat still in his tree, the gun trained on the animal. He had seen deer stagger away after appearing to be mortally wounded. He knew this buck was going to die but he watched down the barrel anyway. He watched it struggle to lift its head. Front hooves clawing at the duff, trying to raise up. Not long though. Most of its body was unresponsive and finally the deer just laid its head down.

It had been born in these bluffs. Sustained by the sun's rays and water and dirt together transmuted to green matter and then to milk. It had come to this point by conducting itself with great caution and care and observation which in sum begat certain behavior and a logging of events in time. All the while a body of the forest; not mining its fertility but rather living within it. Now at the shoulder of the gully everything it had seen and smelled and heard; any such memories or understandings stored away in various recesses ran out invisibly into the leaf litter or the air or wherever they end up. Maybe they went to gray somehow and the deer sensed this fading. This coming apart. A loosening and dispersing. Or maybe everything just winked out to black.

A deer could regard him with penetrating knowing eyes and Bass could destroy its working biology to sustain his own. He never attempted to acquit himself of any such specific act because that wasn't the talking or thinking point. Dreams of innocence are only dreams his father had told him. All forms destined to become dust and rise again as some other. Bass lowered the gun and watched the stilled deer. When he was sure it was dead he stepped down the tree and crossed the gully.

Cyprinus

Scanning ahead was always the reminder put forward by John Bass. Too often the tendency was to burn one's eyes into the water in an immediate radius. But spotting fish at a good distance allows for calculation and design of the best approach and so Bass always reminded and Cloutier always listened. On this day the dark shapes were occasionally obvious but often the anglers were not afforded high contrast imagery. Sometimes subtle color differences, nervous water, varying grayness or obscure linearity were the only indications.

The men walked side by side in a loose rank downriver. In a back corner off the main current Cloutier spotted a carp. He studied the fish while Bass pointed at it and urged him forward. The next consideration was executing an angle of approach that provided for the best presentation. Cloutier also weighed carefully the allowable closeness of his stalk. Carp feel water pushed at them. They feel the sounds of boots on cobble. The men were regularly foiled by carp that perceived their presence before a stalk could even be initiated. These understandings shaped his path and brought him to an increasingly lower crouch as Cloutier moved forward.

The fish was tailing in thigh-deep water. The men could now see the carp clearly. The task at hand was presenting a fly without spooking the quarry with a too-heavy plop or tippet across the dorsal. The fly must be in the feeding cone of the individual fish,

as they do not grant favors. They do not move much and they would never be so coarse as to strike a fly, Bass had told him once: they eat, they don't strike. Put the fly where it needs to be or walk away stoned.
Cloutier presented the fly with sufficient and practiced care and counted it down according to a known sink rate. He was focused on the fish, looking for tells. There would be nothing obvious. Only subtleties: changes in the angle of inclination, hurrying of the tail motion, barely-discernable head turns sometimes on the longitudinal axis. This puts the burden of detection on the angler. That burden is at once physical, technical and religious because the setting of the hook often constitutes an act of faith. Bass and Cloutier had gotten into their heads the fact that flies will be eaten by carp even when the sum of all visual evidence falls short of confirmation.

Cloutier picked up the soft hackle and cast it again, sinking it at a forty-five-degree angle maybe six inches from the tipped-down carp. He perceived what he believed was an eat but set the hook to no connection. The carp started moving off; not blown but moving off slowly. Cloutier set out an intercept cast based on the fish's rate of travel, the depth of the water and the fly's sink rate. An estimation employed. When the fish touched the plane scrolled by the falling fly Cloutier picked up the rod. Damn it if that fish didn't eat he said. Bass exclaimed something similar and smiled, both men watching the hooked carp take line and head for the main river.

Rainbow Inn

A man came from inside the bar or somewhere behind the building. He was moving in a skulking crouch and muttering who wants to scrap. I heard someone wants to scrap. Bass and Cloutier and a number of companions turned to study the newcomer but that was his design and in that moment of pause the assaulter executed on one of the men a kick to the left shin followed by a right roundhouse punch. This too was a calculated sequence: when the wounded party bent forward at the kick his face pushed out as target for the punch. The blow broke the man's two front teeth and he held his mouth and moved to the side of the group humming through his fingers.

What the hell said Cloutier and he and several others braced themselves but generally stood their ground. Another bigger man came out of the building. A ruffian in a sleeveless shirt overlain by cheap jeweled chains. I heard there were some Millers out here he said. He grasped the neck of one Miller and pushed the smaller man to the cracked black of the parking lot. I fuckin hate Millers he said and ground the man's face into the pavement.

Bass and Cloutier stared at Miller. They tensed but then looked up when the first scrapper asked after the biggest son of a bitch out here and started at a man named Dickson. Dickson was indeed a big man but he was overcome by the unpausing

aggressor who gave him one deep hard uppercut to the gut.
Dickson doubled over and stumbled. He nearly fell to the ground but managed to stagger away and lean against a battered pickup truck. At this point someone yelled something about local authorities or the barkeep or other men unknown approaching. This sent the first assaulter running low and hard away from the group around the back of the building. He ran with his head and shoulders down and his eyes wide casting side to side like a transgressor for whom justice was coming.

The man who held Miller let him loose and stood up. No one said anything. Miller lay on the pavement. The sleeveless man walked away without urgency. The group stood the parking lot each man poised but motionless.

Neither Bass nor Cloutier nor any man had taken action to help their companions. They would each come to think about this in all years following: think about how it might have gone otherwise. Bass would learn that thoughtful and careful men are often overwhelmed by raw aggression. They wait to see. The moment passes.

Windbreak

In back of the old granary that'd been converted to a simple cabin they walked the windbreak. Two rows of spruce. At the west end they found black crow feathers ringing each conifer like some dark permanent tears loosely accumulated. Bass brought a feather to the man who took it and moved his thumb and finger along the quill and showed him how the barbs come apart and then sew back together. He remarked on the feather calling it both elegant and utilitarian. Bass didn't know the word utilitarian but he understood when the man said that given all the resources in the world people couldn't make anything so beautiful and useful all at once. Bass asked about tying flies of all black and the man confirmed it would indeed work: they could catch fish using flies made from nothing but crow. The man bent to gather some himself and when he turned back to the boy he found him crying. The boy standing with arms at sides and eyes downcast gently crying. What is it asked the man. What is it. Bass said I'm going to be so scared when you die. The man set his hands on the boy's shoulders. The rows of spruce and no sound other than the careful sobbing. The man said there's a lot more to come before that happens and he spoke to the boy or to himself or both. He held the boy and said that it's not often you can find so many crow feathers in one place and he asked the boy if he knew why the feathers were there; if he remembered another such place. They boy did remember and they talked about walking into their deerstands through an old plantation. In the very dark morning hours. Crows all roosted in the spruce and pine trees. They recalled being startled the first few times but then coming to expect them: black birds and black calls pushing off into dark around. At these memories Bass stopped crying but did not raise his eyes. The man handed what feathers he had found to Bass. Then together they went about collecting more.

Acknowledgements

Some of these poems have been previously published in the following journals, newspapers and anthologies: Minneapolis *Star Tribune, Poetic Strokes, Crossings at Zumbrota's Poet & Artist Collaboration, The Lindenwood Review, Lost Lake Folk Opera, Green Blade, The Lake, The Talking Stick* (various editions). Poems included in the section, *In Falling Red Pines,* are reprinted with permission from Red Dragonfly Press.

About the Author

Justin Watkins was born in the top right corner of Minnesota and now lives with his wife and two sons in the bottom right corner of the state. He walks trout streams, wades carp flats and paddles with family and friends. He graduated from St. Olaf College in 1998. His chapbook, *Bottom Right Corner*, won the 2014 Red Dragonfly Press Emergence Chapbook Competition.

Up On Big Rock Poetry Series
SHIPWRECKT BOOKS PUBLISHING COMPANY
Minnesota

Made in the USA
Monee, IL
14 July 2021

72861607R00083